WASTES

WASTES

CHRISTINA G. MILLER
AND
LOUISE A. BERRY

FRANKLIN WATTS
NEW YORK/LONDON/TORONTO/SYDNEY/1986
A FIRST BOOK

Permission to reuse diagram on p. 17
courtesy of S.D. Warren Company.
Permission to reuse diagram on p. 26
courtesy of The New Book of Popular Science © 1982 Grolier.

Diagrams by Corinne Hekker.

Photographs courtesy of
UPI/Bettmann Newsphotos: pp. 5, 9, 14, 46;
American Iron and Steel Institute: p. 12;
The Bettmann Archive: pp. 20, 23;
EPA/Steve Delaney: p. 28;
New England Aquarium/Bill Wasserman: pp. 40, 41;
The City of San Diego Water Utilities Department: p. 53.

Library of Congress Cataloging in Publication Data
Miller, Christina G.
Wastes.

(A First book)
Includes index.
Summary: Surveys the treatment of household waste
and some possible future solutions to the growing
problem of its disposal.
1. Refuse and refuse disposal—United States—
Juvenile literature. (1. Refuse and refuse disposal)
I. Berry, Louise A.   II. Title.
TD792.M55   1986   363.7'28   85-22653
ISBN 0-531-10130-4

CONTENTS

ACKNOWLEDGMENTS

We wish to thank the following people for being valuable resources to us as we researched the material for this book.

The staff of the Environmental Science and Natural History Departments, Massachusetts Audubon Society Headquarters, Lincoln, Massachusetts

Dr. Les Kaufman, Curator of Education, New England Aquarium, Boston, Massachusetts

Benedict R. Schwegler, Jr., Project Engineer, Research and Development, WED Enterprises, Glendale, California

K. Gary Stevens, Plant Superintendent, Padre Dam Municipal Water District, Santee, California

1

JUST WHAT ARE HOUSEHOLD WASTES?

Every day everyone throws lots of things "away." For most of us, once things we want to get rid of are out of sight, they are also out of mind. But have you ever wondered what happens to the water flushed down the toilet, or trash and garbage emptied into the garbage truck?

Household wastes are made up of *sewage*, the wastes and water that are flushed or go down the drain, and *solid wastes*, the garbage and trash. People are becoming concerned about the quantity of wastes, as well as the kind of wastes, we are producing. Beautiful and useful land is being turned into ugly garbage heaps, and originally clear, clean waters are becoming too polluted to drink or to be used for recreation. We are learning that when we dispose of wastes, there is really no such place as "away" on planet Earth.

SOLID WASTES

Each of us generates a minimum of a barrel or can of trash a week. Some kinds of wastes that we produce are too large to fit into a trash container, but are also part of the *wastestream.* Old bicycles, mattresses, rugs, furniture, refrigerators, and washing machines are but a few examples. In the United

States, about 200 million automobile tires are discarded every year. In 1985, solid wastes in our country alone were estimated to weigh 6.6 billion tons (5.94 billion metric tons).

SEWAGE

Each of our bodies produces less than 100 gallons (380 l) of urine a year. But we each create more than 8,000 gallons (30,400 l) of sewage a year just by using the flush toilet. With each flush, the toilet uses five gallons (19 l) of clean water, which then becomes *wastewater,* to carry away our very small amount of bodily wastes. Wastewater is also generated when we use sinks, dishwashers, washing machines, garbage disposals, bathtubs, and showers.

WASTE PRODUCTS
IN NATURE

Wastes are produced not only by human beings, but also by all other living things as well. Everything from the tiniest microscopic plant in the woods to the great whales of the ocean produces waste products. Yet we are not aware of them as we walk along a woodland path or swim in the sea. Why don't all the leaves, pinecones, evergreen needles, and branches that have fallen in a forest throughout time form a pile of brush as high as the treetops? Where are the cracked eggs of the birds that have hatched, the shells from the nuts that squirrels and chipmunks have eaten, and the animal manure? What has happened to bodies of birds, insects, and animals that have died and the snakeskin that has been shed? Although these waste products seem to have disappeared as if by magic, nature has actually recycled them.

Fallen leaves, animal wastes, and even dead plants and animals are reused in nature. Decomposers are organisms which recycle by using dead plants and animals for food. They include bacteria, millipedes, ants, earthworms, slugs, and other organisms. They obtain food by breaking down dead plants and animals and waste materials into their basic chemicals. Elements such as carbon, nitrogen, phosphorus, and potassium are returned to the soil through the decomposers' waste products and bodies when they die. Living plants take up these minerals through their roots and use them to grow. This is why forests do not need to be fertilized. They are part of nature's great recycling system, which uses all wastes as resources.

Another of nature's recyclers is the American dung beetle. These scaly insects feed on the dung of deer. Some species of birds use others' waste products in different ways. Built into the nest of the tufted titmouse is the fur of the possum. The tree swallow lines its nest with fallen bird feathers, and the great crested flycatcher constructs its nest of snakeskin.

WHAT'S IN TRASH

What happens to the trash which people discard? Let's pretend that we are archeologists who many years in the future find the trash we discarded today. What might have been thrown away? The list is endless. Perhaps there would be Styrofoam cups, newspapers, beverage cans, broken plastic toys, cracked drinking glasses, twist-off bottle caps, "disposable" diapers, razor blades, and scratched phonograph records. Some things would be almost impossible to recognize. A newspaper would be *decomposed*. A razor blade would be rusty and full of holes. A glass might be broken into smaller pieces, but would still be recognizable. The plastic items would look just about the same.

The wastestream items that break down and decompose are *biodegradable*. Natural substances are biodegradable, but the time they take to decompose varies greatly. A newspaper, for example, breaks down very rapidly; the glass, however, may take centuries. Plastics, on the other hand, are made from chemicals in an industrial process. They are nonbiodegradable and therefore cannot be broken down by decomposers. Although they will break into smaller pieces, they will never return to the basic materials from which scientists made them in a laboratory.

The plastics and other kinds of solid wastes we generate are just part of the disposal problem. We are also producing more wastes in the United States today than ever before in our nation's history. Because of the abundance of available goods and our ability to buy them, Americans not only enjoy one of the highest standards of living in the world, but also produce the most wastes.

OUR "THROWAWAY" SOCIETY

Because we use items briefly and then throw them away, we are rapidly depleting our limited supply of natural resources. Our civilization has been described as a "throwaway" society. It is only recently that we have begun to question whether there will always be enough raw materials for our way of life to continue without change. Americans are only about 5 percent of the world's population, yet we use 40 percent of the world's natural resources. As developing nations grow, they will increase their demand for natural resources too.

The idea of planned obsolescence has become a way of life for Americans. The word *obsolete* means outmoded or no longer in use. When the phrase "planned obsolescence" is applied to products, it means that they are designed not to be durable and long-lasting but to wear out in a relatively short time or to be replaced by another product that performs the same function better or in a different way. For example, automobiles could be designed to last much longer than they

How we waste our natural resources can be seen here when a sanitation workers' strike caused garbage to pile up on the sidewalks of New York City. In addition to kitchen wastes there are plastic, paper, metal, and cloth products, visible reminders of our "throwaway" society.

do. However, they are built so that they will have to be replaced frequently. Other products, such as clothing, may be designed to go out of style even while they are still useful. Often the cost of repairing a broken appliance, such as an iron, may be greater than the cost of purchasing a new one. Replacement parts or repair services may not even be available. When old products are frequently replaced with new, a great volume of solid wastes is created, and our supply of natural resources shrinks.

We have come to realize that our environment does not have an unlimited capacity to absorb all the wastes that we produce without becoming polluted. Today scientists are studying how to dispose of society's wastes without harming the environment. You are probably familiar with some of the solutions, such as recycling. However, you may be surprised by some of the new methods that are being used to obtain resources from wastes.

2

TRACKING
THE
TRASH

Today the disposal of solid wastes in the United States is a major concern. Not only has the population more than doubled in the past fifty years, but the amount of solid waste each person generates has also greatly increased. (We generate enough solid wastes in the United States every day to fill the New Orleans Superdome from floor to ceiling twice.) Because of the increasing amount of solid wastes, the greater cost of the land used as disposal sites, the longer distances trash collectors must travel to the sites, and the cost of protective measures that must now to be taken to safeguard the environment, waste disposal has become very expensive.

SOLID WASTE DISPOSAL
IN THE PAST

The problems posed by solid wastes have been apparent for centuries. In ancient Greece and Rome, large numbers of people lived in cities. As a result, a great amount of solid wastes was produced in a small land area. Although the Romans designed advanced water and sewer systems, they dumped most of their garbage and trash in large open pits at the edge of the city. These first dumps were unsightly, smelly, and attracted flies and rats.

During the late Middle Ages (1000–1500 A.D.) in Europe, garbage disposal was even more primitive than in Roman times. People simply opened their doors and windows and threw wastes outside. City dwellers who lived near rivers and harbors discarded their wastes in the water. Filthy streets and water made living conditions unhealthy, and tens of thousands of people died from plagues.

In our own country in the 1800s, as large numbers of farmers moved to cities to work in factories, getting rid of wastes in these high-population areas became a problem. How were all the garbage, manure, wastepaper, wood and coal ashes, old shoes, rusty tin cans, and other things to be disposed of? Much of this *refuse* was dumped in the nearest vacant lot. Some city governments hired trash collectors to haul rubbish to open dumps at the city's edge. There, among the heaps of rotting garbage, loose papers blew in the wind and fires often started spontaneously from the heat produced by decaying matter. These dumps, like those of ancient times, attracted disease carriers, such as rats, flies, and mosquitoes.

In some cities, garbage composed of food wastes was collected separately and transported to a central location called a "swill yard." There it was carted away by hog farmers to feed to their pigs. Some of these animals became ill from eating the rotten garbage, and died of hog cholera. Others developed trichinosis, a disease which can be passed on to people who eat infested meat that has not been fully cooked. For health reasons, the feeding of raw garbage to pigs was later outlawed in many countries.

Garbage barges are loaded at a sanitation department facility on the Hudson River in New York City; from here they are hauled to landfills. Before restrictive legislation was passed, the garbage was simply transported a few miles offshore and dumped in the ocean.

The rest of the city's solid wastes were often loaded onto barges called "garbage scows," which were pulled by tugboats into lakes, rivers, and oceans. The city of Chicago's solid wastes were dumped into Lake Michigan; garbage from New Orleans was dumped into the Mississippi River; and eastern coastal cities, such as New York, dumped their wastes into the Atlantic Ocean. However, garbage from New York City often washed up on New Jersey beaches along with the incoming tides. In 1933, in a lawsuit filed by the State of New Jersey against the City of New York, the United States Supreme Court ruled there could be no more dumping of refuse into water.

As concern about disposing of wastes on land and water mounted, sanitary engineers sought other solutions. At first, burning wastes at high temperatures was thought to be a suitable method of getting rid of it. Cities built large incinerators to burn garbage and trash. New apartment buildings were equipped with trash chutes. Rubbish emptied into the chutes collected in the basement and was burned in a small incinerator. Incinerators of all sizes spewed forth clouds of dark smoke from their chimneys. Black soot covered windowsills and the outsides of buildings. Not until the passage of the Clean Air Act and its amendments during the 1960s and 1970s were many of these incinerators closed down. The new law required pollution controls that made the continued operation of the incinerators too costly.

SOLID WASTE
DISPOSAL TODAY

In 1976, in a major effort to protect the environment, Congress passed the Resource Conservation and Recovery Act, which set strict standards for disposal of solid wastes.

In the past, wetlands were used as places to dump trash because people did not realize the value of these areas. They thought of them as useless land, not recognizing their importance to migrating waterfowl.

Dumping in wetlands created more direct problems for humans, too, because *leachate*, the liquid which may seep out of dumps, may contain hazardous substances, such as motor oil, improperly disposed of at the dump. Underground streams or rainwater can carry the leachate to wells or reservoirs, making the water unsafe to drink.

The Resource Conservation and Recovery Act also prohibits dumping in salt marshes, which are coastal areas where fresh and salt water meet. Before this law was passed, wetlands were filled with solid wastes to form dry land. The stadium where the New York Giants play is built on the site of a former salt marsh. Today we know that salt marshes serve as nurseries for fish and other marine life.

How do we dispose of all our great quantities of wastes in accordance with laws recently passed to protect our environment? When you put something in the trash, what happens to it? In some cities and towns, individuals are responsible for taking their own solid wastes to a sanitary landfill or to a waste transfer station. This is a central collection point where some sorting and compacting may be done. In other cities and towns trucks collect rubbish from curbsides, where it is placed in barrels or trash bags by residents. Then the rubbish is taken to sanitary landfills for burial or to incinerators, where it is burned.

SANITARY LANDFILLS

Environmental planners hoped that sanitary landfills would provide enough space for the huge amount of solid wastes we generate while eliminating problems associated with open dumps. Their planning and designs take into account soil and water conditions and characteristics of the land. In one kind of landfill a deep trench is dug. After the refuse is deposited, a bulldozer is used to cover it with soil. In another method, the refuse is buried in an existing quarry or ravine. The covering layer of earth prevents rats from boring, insect eggs from hatching, and odors from escaping. *Microorganisms* break down the organic refuse in a natural chemical reaction which causes the temperature within the landfill to rise. This also helps to kill most of the disease-causing bacteria.

The soil covering the refuse in a sanitary landfill contains

microorganisms called *aerobes*. They use the air in the soil to decompose materials in the sanitary landfill. When all of the air in the soil has been used up, other microorganisms, called *anaerobes*, which live in the absence of air, continue to feed on the refuse. This produces several gases: carbon dioxide; ammonia; methane, which is similar to natural gas; and hydrogen sulfide, which smells like rotten eggs. The process of decomposition continues for many years.

When the sanitary landfill is full, it is closed, and the land can be used for other purposes. Because the methane gas that is produced in a sanitary landfill can explode if it builds up in a confined space, and because landfills continue to shift and settle as wastes decay, buildings cannot be safely constructed over a sanitary landfill unless special provisions are made. Often instead the land is planted with grass and used for parks, playgrounds, golf courses, or ball fields. In Virginia Beach, Virginia, the pile of solid wastes at a sanitary landfill became so high that it was landscaped to be used as a ski slope in the winter. It is named Mount Trashmore.

DUMPS

In spite of strict regulatory laws, dumps still exist in many places, particularly in rural areas and in the western United States. Sanitary landfills in these sparsely populated areas are often so far away that they are inconvenient to use. Even if the garbage is disposed of separately from the trash, some food scraps find their way to the dump. As little as one-quarter of a teaspoon of food remaining in a tin can will be enough to attract rats. Bears and raccoons, and some birds, also forage for food at open dumps. Screeching gulls circling overhead can often be seen near dumps.

This garbage is being dumped into a long conveyer machine which shreds it for reuse in a landfill.

Hungry sea gulls flock to this garbage
dump on the California coast.

INCINERATORS AND
RESOURCE
RECOVERY PLANTS

In some cities, there is not enough land to bury all the solid wastes that are produced. Instead, wastes are incinerated in large furnaces which reach temperatures between 1600° and 1900° F (871° and 1037° C). The material that will burn is reduced to carbon dioxide and other gases and to ash. The ash, which weighs from one-quarter to one-fifth of the original wastes, is then trucked to a sanitary landfill, where it is buried. Incinerators are expensive to build and are complex to operate. Furthermore, burning trash can be harmful to the environment if incinerators do not have adequate air-pollution control devices. Even with these controls, it is possible for small amounts of dangerous pollutants to be discharged into the air.

In the early 1970s, when the United States was in the midst of a severe fuel-oil shortage, specially designed incinerators called resource recovery plants were planned. It was hoped that by burning garbage as fuel, these plants could help lessen both the energy and the solid wastes crises. The heat produced by burning wastes would be converted to steam, which could then be used for several purposes: to heat and cool buildings, to generate electricity, to power the plant's fans and pumps, or to heat water. Usable materials, such as iron, glass, and aluminum, which remained in the ash after the burning process, would be separated and sold to industries which would make them into new products.

In 1981 only twenty-nine resource recovery plants were operating in the United States. Many of the waste management companies that own these facilities have found that selling the energy they produce has not always been profitable. However, they do make money from the sale of metals and glass separated from the ash, and from "tipping fees." This is the money refuse companies pay to empty their trucks at the resource recovery plant.

One successful resource recovery plant in Saugus, Massachusetts, has been operating since 1973. It receives solid wastes from eighteen municipalities. After the solid wastes are collected, they are transported by truck to the plant. There they are weighed and discharged into a large storage pit. Overhead cranes then scoop up the wastes and deposit them into the hopper of a furnace. Within the furnace, the wastes tumble through a series of three grates as they burn. Gases pass through devices specially designed to control air emissions. Large magnets remove scrap iron from the ash. The resource recovery plant in Saugus sells its steam to the General Electric Company. The use of the energy has saved millions of barrels of oil.

Resource recovery plants are being considered again by some large cities. Sanitary engineers in New York City plan to build two facilities to process some of the quantities of garbage that city produces every year. Estimates are that by the year 2000, Fresh Kills, the city's sanitary landfill, which is the largest in the world, will be full and that the mountain of garbage at this site will be several hundred feet high. The city of Chicago's Northwest Waste-to-Energy Facility incinerates some of the city's solid wastes, and additional facilities are planned.

HAZARDOUS WASTE DISPOSAL

Hazardous wastes present special disposal problems. There are many hazardous products we use in our houses and yards which, if disposed of unwisely, can harm wildlife and could contaminate drinking-water supplies. These include turpentine, paint, antifreeze, drain cleaners, swimming pool chemicals, wood stains, preservatives, varnishes, chemical fertilizers, and weed and insect control chemicals. By law, industries must pay for the disposal of their large volumes of hazardous wastes at licensed hazardous waste management facilities. However, it would be very expensive to transport small quantities of hazardous household wastes to approved sites. Consequently, hazardous household wastes are frequently added to the trash or stored in garages, basements, or toolsheds for long periods of time.

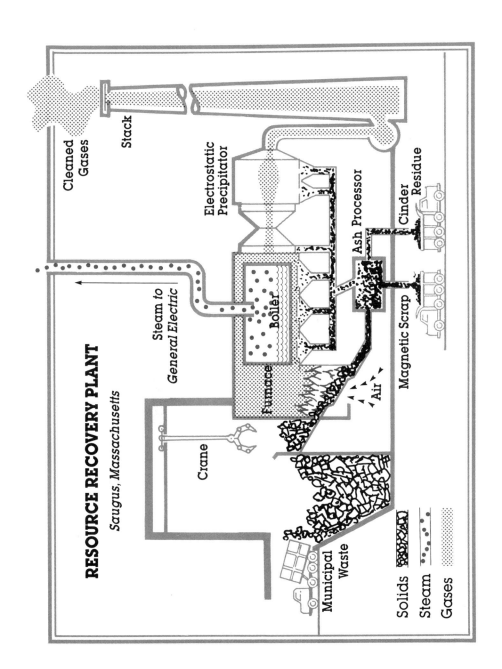

RESOURCE RECOVERY PLANT
Saugus, Massachusetts

Cleaned Gases

Stack

Electrostatic Precipitator

Steam *to* General Electric

Boiler

Furnace

Crane

Air

Ash Processor

Magnetic Scrap

Cinder Residue

Municipal Waste

Solids
Steam
Gases

Let's look at one town's solution to the problem. In 1982, residents of Lexington, Massachusetts, became concerned about hazardous wastes being kept in places where pets or young children could reach them. Interested citizens invited the town's fire chief, along with the heads of the Board of Health, the Department of Public Works, and the Conservation Commission, to form a committee to study the problem of household hazardous waste disposal. Later, other experts, such as safety engineers in industry, chemists, and a licensed hazardous wastes hauler, joined the group. The proposed solution was a one-day collection of hazardous wastes at a central location in the town. Since Lexington was one of the first communities in the United States to collect household hazardous wastes, lawyers studied who would pay the costs if someone were injured, and arranged for insurance. Permission had to be obtained from town officials and from state and federal governments as well. In addition to the town's setting aside money, local businesses contributed to pay for the hazardous wastes collection. Posters displayed in supermarkets, banks, stores, and libraries advertised the hazardous wastes pickup, which was scheduled for a Saturday in October at the Public Works Department yard.

As the day approached, the organizers began to wonder if anyone would come. However, it turned out to be a beautiful New England autumn day, and even before the ten o'clock start, people began lining up with their buckets of paint and cans of insect sprays. Newspaper reporters and television crews recorded how people handed over their materials to a chemist who asked them to identify the contents. Then an employee of the disposal company sorted the wastes into chemically compatible groups and packed them in special barrels for transportation to the disposal site. Some of the subtances would be recycled and others would be disposed of by incineration or burial at a special landfill.

Lexington's household hazardous wastes project was so successful that it has been repeated every year and has become a model program for other communities throughout the United States.

3

WHERE DOES THE SEWAGE GO?

Ever since the first people lived on earth, they have had to dispose of their bodily wastes and wastewater. Methods of disposal have changed throughout history to meet each society's needs. Cave men and women did not have toilets; they simply eliminated wherever the need arose. If they used water for washing, it could be dumped almost anywhere.

The first plumbing systems were developed to dispose of human wastes. One of the earliest of these was built between 2000 B.C. and 1500 B.C. at the palace of King Minos at Knossos on the Mediterranean island of Crete. Rainwater collected on the roof and flowed through a series of earthenware pipes to a toilet in the queen's bathroom. There it was used to carry away feces and urine. (Archeologists have also found a clay bathtub shaped like bathtubs of today.)

Bathing and personal tidiness were very important to people in ancient Greece and Rome. (Hygeia was the goddess of health in Greek mythology. It is from her name that the word *hygiene* comes. It means the practice of cleanliness and the preservation of health.) Large public Roman baths contained a series of rooms. After leaving the dressing room, Romans bathed first in cool water and gradually progressed to warmer pools, finally arriving at a steam bath. Then, a plunge into a

In the Roman baths, the bather,
after leaving the dressing room,
progressed through a series of rooms,
bathing first in cool water, and
gradually moving on to warmer pools,
finally arriving at a steam bath.
The bather completed the ritual by
plunging into a pool of cold water.

pool of cold water completed the bath. The many gallons of water required for the baths were brought from distant mountain springs by long channels called *aqueducts.*

Wealthy Romans constructed latrines on the ground level of their dwellings. If an aqueduct was nearby, water could be used to carry waste into the sewers which, in Rome, drained into the Tiber River. Public latrines were built along sewer routes.

In contrast to the ancient Greeks and Romans, Europeans during the Middle Ages did not bathe often. They thought hygiene was of little importance. In London, England, household wastewater, garbage, and stable wastes were dumped into open ditches, which teemed with flies and rats and bore the stench of rotting matter. Eventually these ditches flowed to the Thames River. Some castles and monasteries had simple latrines built into the outer walls, and wastes drained into the surrounding moats.

During the nineteenth century, in cities and rural areas, most of the people used backyard outhouses—small wooden shacks housing a privy. Feces and urine collected in a metal pail, which was emptied into a container in the ground called a *cesspit* or privy vault. Drivers of horse drawn vehicles, called "honey wagons," pumped the contents of cesspits into their tank wagons. Because collection occurred largely at night and was usually deposited as fertilizer on land, these wastes became known as "night soil."

Until about a century ago, houses in the United States were built without indoor bathrooms. Outhouses continued to be in use. It was not until 1830 that water became available in many American cities and people began having it piped into their houses.

Although there were no bathrooms, commodes and washstands were often located in the bedrooms. A washstand was a wooden structure holding a washbowl, mirror, and towel rails. Water was carried to it in a pitcher from the only faucet in the house—most commonly in the kitchen. A commode had a wooden seat with a bucket beneath it to contain human wastes.

Because bathing was inconvenient, it was usually done only once a week. The "Saturday night bath" usually occurred in the kitchen. Water was heated on the stove and poured into a metal tub which was brought into the room for the occasion.

The first sewage systems in European and American cities were constructed in the mid-nineteenth century. These systems were designed to carry only rainwater and prevent it from collecting in the streets. About the same time, with the availability of running water, commodes and outhouses began to be replaced by water closets, a type of privy which had a hand pump connected to a small container of water. Water, pumped into the latrine, carried human wastes, by pipe, to a cesspit.

The increased volume of wastes which resulted from the addition of water caused cesspits and privy vaults to overflow. Sometimes sewage seeped into wells and other sources of drinking water. Very little was known about how diseases were spread from one person to another. Contaminated drinking water caused the deaths of thousands of people from such diseases as cholera, typhoid, and enteric fever.

When the public became more aware of the health hazards of raw sewage, people asked their city governments to allow householders to connect water closets directly to sewers. In some municipalities, such as Chicago, Illinois, and the borough of Brooklyn, New York, this was permitted.

THE FLUSH TOILET

The modern toilet of today developed from an invention made by a plumber, Thomas Crapper, who was born in England in 1837. He invented the flush toilet valve, which made water a

Water closets preceded the modern flush toilet. This advertisement of the 1800s is for an institutional-type water closet for use in schools.

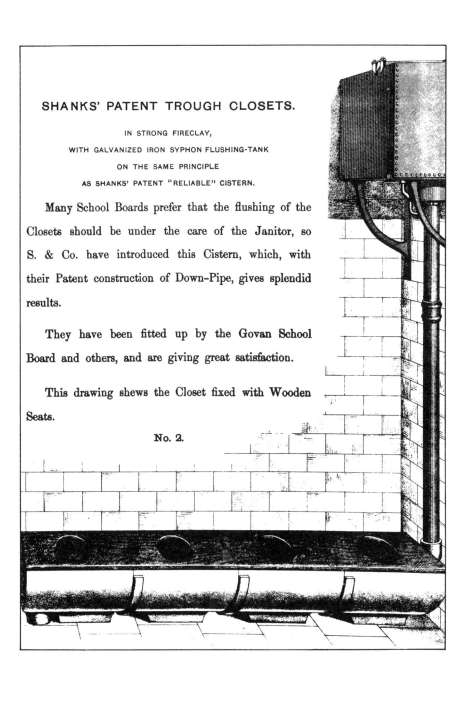

SHANKS' PATENT TROUGH CLOSETS.

IN STRONG FIRECLAY,
WITH GALVANIZED IRON SYPHON FLUSHING-TANK
ON THE SAME PRINCIPLE
AS SHANKS' PATENT "RELIABLE" CISTERN.

Many School Boards prefer that the flushing of the Closets should be under the care of the Janitor, so S. & Co. have introduced this Cistern, which, with their Patent construction of Down-Pipe, gives splendid results.

They have been fitted up by the Govan School Board and others, and are giving great satisfaction.

This drawing shews the Closet fixed with Wooden Seats.

No. 2.

more practical transporter of human wastes. A tank high above the toilet contained clean water for flushing. When a chain was pulled, Crapper's valve released the water, which flowed by gravity into the toilet bowl. The water carried the wastes out of the toilet bowl and into a pipe which was connected to the sewage system.

Since the invention of the flush toilet and the increased number of sinks, showers, bathtubs, washing machines, dishwashers, and other water-utilizing devices, the amount of water people use has increased dramatically. It is estimated that each person in the United States creates 100 gallons (380 l) of wastewater each day. Because we use so much water, some experts fear there will be a shortage of clean drinking water in the future.

COMBINED AND
SEPARATE
SEWER SYSTEMS

When wastewater leaves your household, it enters a sewage system. There are two basic kinds. Sewage systems that combine rainwater and household wastewater are called combined systems. These were built and remain in use in some cities, such as Boston, Massachusetts, and New York City.

When separate systems are used, there are two sets of pipes underground. One carries rainwater to nearby rivers and streams and the other carries sewage to treatment plants. It was not until 1880, in Memphis, Tennessee, that the first sewage system providing for household wastes alone was built. Today, separate systems exist in many cities. They have several advantages over combined systems. When rainwater is put into rivers and streams, it slowly soaks into surrounding wetland areas, which act as sponges and replenish the supply of groundwater. This is the water beneath the ground supplying springs and wells from which drinking water comes. Separate sewer systems, therefore, help to conserve water because rainwater is returned to the ground. Another advantage of separate systems is that less water must be treated at plants where sewage is purified. Because rainwater is kept separate from sewage, it is not necessary to treat it.

THE CLEAN WATER ACT

The intent of the Clean Water Act of 1977 is to restore and maintain purity in our nation's waters. In order to control water pollution this law limited the amount of wastes that can be discharged into waters.

Scientists use several methods to determine the effect sewage will have on the receiving water. One is called BOD, which stands for Biochemical Oxygen Demand. It is a measure of the amount of oxygen in the water that the sewage will use up as it is broken down by decay bacteria. If sewage requires too much oxygen to be broken down, it will deprive fish and other aquatic animals of oxygen needed to live. They will no longer be able to help the water to be pure and it will become polluted.

Scientists also look at samples of water to determine its color and clarity. Cleanest water is clear, colorless, and odorless. In addition, they take samples and examine them under microscopes to count bacteria. *Escherichia coli (E. coli)* are called "indicator organisms" because they indicate the presence of disease-causing microorganisms in the water. *E. coli* live in the intestines of humans and other warm-blooded animals. The number of *E. coli* is one indication of the water's purity—the greater the number of *E. coli,* the less pure the water.

CENTRALIZED
SEWAGE SYSTEMS

Various levels of treatment (primary, secondary, and tertiary) are used to purify sewage. Sometimes a special permit allows only primary treatment, but usually sewage is required to have a minimum of the first two levels of treatment. All of these three treatment processes separate sewage into effluent and sludge. *Effluent* is the liquid wastewater; *sludge* is the sediment that

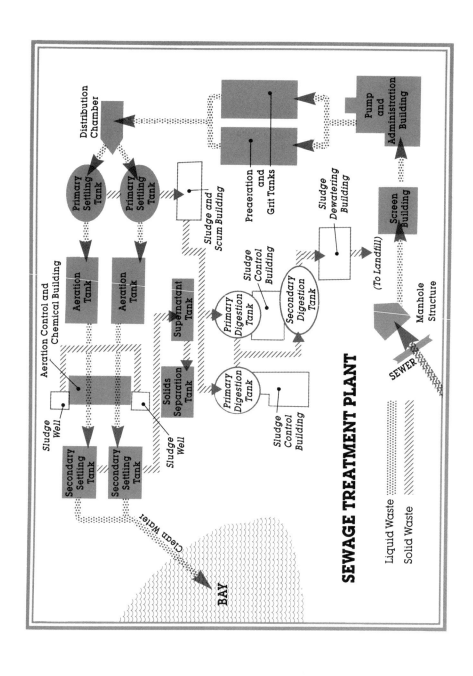

SEWAGE TREATMENT PLANT

Distribution Chamber

Primary Settling Tank

Primary Settling Tank

Aeration Control and Chemical Building

Aeration Tank

Aeration Tank

Sludge Well

Secondary Settling Tank

Secondary Settling Tank

Sludge and Scum Building

Supernatant Tank

Solids Separation Tank

Sludge Well

Primary Digestion Tank

Sludge Control Building

Secondary Digestion Tank

Primary Digestion Tank

Sludge Control Building

Preaeration and Grit Tanks

Pump and Administration Building

Sludge Dewatering Building

Screen Building

(To Landfill)

Manhole Structure

SEWER

BAY

Clean Water

Liquid Waste

Solid Waste

remains in the sewage after the wastewater is removed. The purity of the effluent and sludge improves with each additional level of treatment.

When raw, or untreated, sewage arrives at the treatment plant, it looks and smells foul. Although it is 99 percent water, it usually contains many different things: feces, urine, soap and detergents, chemicals, microorganisms, and a variety of other items, such as vegetable peelings, fruit skins, coffee grounds, toilet paper, and even buttons and cigarette butts. In addition to household wastes, sewage may also contain waste products from factories and businesses.

Primary treatment removes from 40 percent to 50 percent of the solids. First the sewage is passed through coarse wire-mesh screens to remove large items. Next it goes to large tanks called grit chambers, where gravity causes finer materials such as sand to settle to the bottom. The sewage is then pumped to the primary sedimentation tank. While it passes very slowly through this tank, solids which are floating in the water—such as bits of paper and material put through the garbage disposal—sink to the bottom. They form thick, black, slimy sludge. Grease and oil float to the top of the tank and are skimmed off. If the sewage is not going to receive further treatment, it is disinfected with chlorine to kill disease-causing bacteria. Then the effluent is discharged, usually into the ocean. Sunlight, oxygen, and *organisms* which live in salt water continue to purify the effluent.

In secondary treatment, more solids are removed and the resulting effluent is clearer. The most common methods for achieving secondary treatment are the "activated sludge" and the "trickling filtration" processes. In the activated sludge process, sewage is pumped to a tank where it is mixed with oxygen and sludge containing active bacteria. The oxygenated air produces a bubbling action. Useful bacteria multiply and break down the material in the sewage to form simpler, less harmful substances. In the trickling filter process, the tanks are filled with crushed rocks which are covered with slime containing useful bacteria. As the sewage trickles down through

In the secondary-treatment tanks at the
Blue Plains Sewage Waste Treatment Plant in
Washington, D.C., bacteria act on the sewage.

the filter of rocks and slime, the useful bacteria digest harmful bacteria in the sewage.

Tertiary treatment is an advanced form of treatment. It is used after primary and secondary treatment to produce the purest effluent of all treatment levels. It is not used very often because it is expensive and there are very few instances in which such a pure effluent is required. In tertiary treatment, chemicals, microscopic screening, and other methods are employed to produce effluent pure enough to be used in industry, for recreation, and for drinking.

Centralized sewage systems are necessary in cities and towns where many people live and a large volume of sewage is produced. In 1983 public sewage systems in the United States served about 75 percent of the people. The other 25 percent relied on backyard septic tanks and cesspools. In contrast to the United States, more than 70 percent of the world's population have no centralized sewage system.

ON-SITE SEWAGE SYSTEMS

In rural areas, where there is more land, people dispose of wastewater close to where they live. It is not piped to a large, centralized sewage treatment facility. Rather, on-site systems, such as a cesspool or a septic tank, receive wastes from one or very few households or buildings. A cesspool is the more primitive design. It is a large hole dug underground that is lined with either stones, bricks, or concrete blocks. Household wastewater enters the cesspool through a downward-sloping sewage inlet pipe. The liquid part of the raw sewage seeps into the surrounding soil through spaces between the bricks or stones in the cesspool wall, and sludge settles to the bottom. Bacteria cause the gradual breakdown of the cesspool contents.

A septic tank is a watertight concrete, steel, or fiberglass container that is buried underground. Raw sewage flows from a house into the tank through an underground inlet pipe. A vent pipe is connected to the inlet pipe, which allows gases

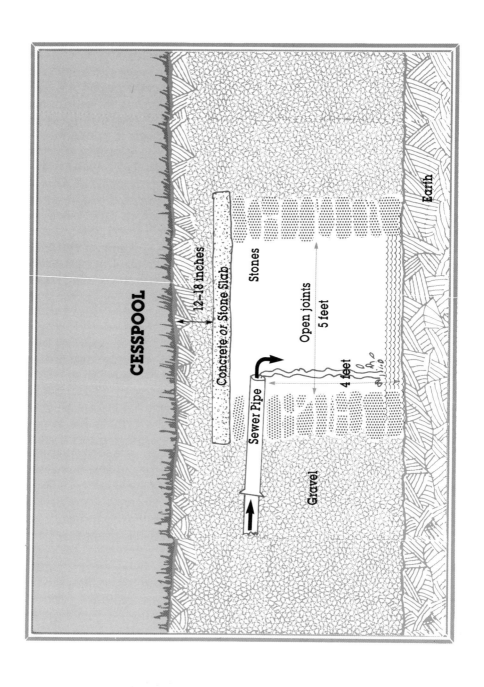

CESSPOOL

12-18 inches

Concrete or Stone Slab

Stones

Open joints

5 feet

4 feet

Sewer Pipe

Gravel

Earth

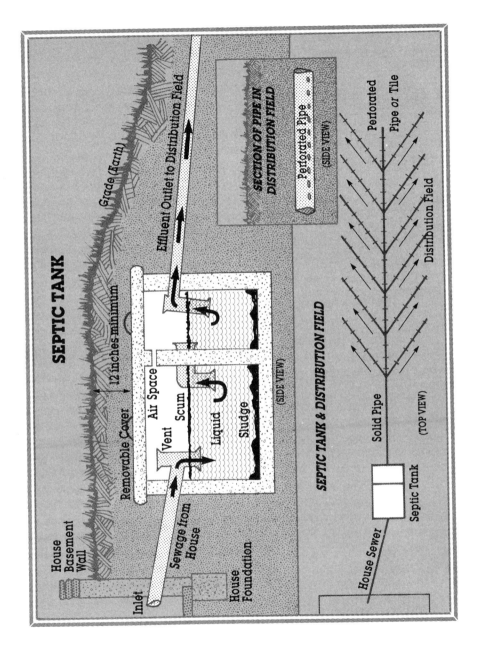

SEPTIC TANK

Grade (Earth)

Effluent Outlet to Distribution Field

12 inches minimum

Removable Cover

House Basement Wall

Inlet

Sewage from House

House Foundation

Air Space

Vent

Scum

Liquid

Sludge

(SIDE VIEW)

SECTION OF PIPE IN DISTRIBUTION FIELD

Perforated Pipe

(SIDE VIEW)

SEPTIC TANK & DISTRIBUTION FIELD

Solid Pipe

House Sewer

Septic Tank

Perforated Pipe or Tile

Distribution Field

(TOP VIEW)

that build up in the septic tank to escape. The heaviest parts of the sewage sink to the bottom of the tank and become sludge. Oil, grease, and other floating material form a thick, foamy scum on the surface of the liquid. Bacteria digest the sludge and scum and change it into a rich mixture of decaying plant and animal matter.

The liquid wastewater flows through an outlet pipe into a leaching field. A leaching field is a large underground area through which a system of pipes runs. The pipes have holes in them which enable the effluent to escape slowly through them and be distributed into the soil. There the decay bacteria in the soil continue to purify the effluent. Before building a septic tank, a "percolation test" is used to determine if the soil provides suitable drainage. To do the test, an engineer pours water into a very small hole in the ground, and measures how fast the water disappears. Soil that is sandy drains faster than soil that contains clay.

Every one to five years, the solid material which remains in cesspools and septic tanks must be pumped out to make more space. The sludge that has collected is pumped through a flexible hose into a specially designed tank truck. It is then transported to a sewage treatment plant.

SLUDGE DISPOSAL

Sludge must be disposed of safely. It still contains harmful bacteria which could cause disease if it came into contact with drinking water supplies. Often sludge is dumped into the ocean or buried in sanitary landfills. There it continues to be broken down through natural processes into less hazardous substances.

The gas sludge gives off as it putrefies is sometimes used as fuel. It is burned and used for generating electricity to operate machinery at treatment plants and to heat settling tanks. In this way, sludge is used as a resource and helps to conserve our limited supplies of coal, oil, and natural gas.

The sludge from some American cities is being used as a fertilizer. It contains nitrogen and phosphorous, elements which are essential for plant growth. If sludge contains no hazardous substances, it can be dried and spread onto land, or it can be used in its liquid form and sprayed onto land. The city of Milwaukee, Wisconsin, sells large bags of its dried sludge throughout the United States. It is called "Milorganite" and is used as fertilizer by gardeners and farmers.

The city of Chicago has had success using its sewage to rebuild land 180 miles (290 km) away which was strip-mined for coal. Sludge is transported by boat down the Illinois River, and then by pipeline to the strip-mined land. When the land is properly rebuilt, the *nutrients* in the sludge will help to grow crops such as corn and soybeans.

4

WASTES
AND
THE
ENVIRONMENT

Solid waste and sewage affect the environment—sometimes in harmful ways. Whether our solid wastes are burned at a resource recovery plant or buried at a sanitary landfill, they can change our environment. If incinerators do not burn properly, they can pollute the air with fly ash, smoke, and harmful gases. With improper incineration, the residue ash emptied out of the resource recovery plant can pollute the sanitary landfill where it is disposed.

NONBIODEGRADABLE
SOLID WASTES

Today most solid wastes are not burned, but are buried at sanitary landfills. Nature does not have the ability to recycle many of these wastes. Packaging materials and other plastics are not biodegradable, which means that they cannot be broken down into harmless, simpler substances by the action of living things.

One reason solid wastes are affecting our environment today is the great increase in packaging materials. When your great-grandparents were your age, many things were sold by bulk rather than in individual containers. A clerk at the general store would scoop out of a large barrel the amount of flour or sugar a customer wanted to buy. Liquids such as vinegar and molasses were drawn out of a keg into a bottle or jug which the customer brought to the store. At the hardware store, nuts, bolts, and nails were kept in bins and sold by weight. Pharmacists made their own "tooth powders," cough syrups, ointments, and salves. When a customer bought fish at the market, it was wrapped in newspaper. Food was usually canned at home in glass jars which were reused each year. The few metal cans that were used were saved to store collections of small items such as buttons or screws or to start seedlings in the early spring. A couple of trips to the dump were all that most families needed to make in a year.

About 35 percent of the solid wastestream coming from households is made up of packages and packaging materials. Let's look at the contents of one bag of groceries to see what is included.* There is:

1 large paper grocery bag
3 qts. milk
3 small plastic-coated cartons (milk)
1 large plastic-coated carton (milk)
cornflakes
1 box (cornflakes)
1 waxed-paper bag (cornflakes)
1 head lettuce
1 Styrofoam tray (lettuce)
1 piece plastic wrap (lettuce)
2 pork chops
1 Styrofoam tray (pork chops)
1 piece plastic wrap (pork chops)
50 ml toothpaste
1 plastic tube (toothpaste)
1 plastic lid (toothpaste)

*From "The Great Garbage Machine," developed by the Waste Management Advisory Board, Ministry of the Environment, Toronto, Ontario, Canada.

1 box (toothpaste)
1 lb. butter
1 piece foil wrap (butter)
1 qt. orange juice
1 qt. glass jar (orange juice)
1 metal top (orange juice)

However, the actual items that were purchased were only:

milk
cornflakes
lettuce
pork chops
toothpaste
butter
juice

Everything else was packaging! Although this is important in keeping food sanitary and preventing spoilage, excess packaging is a waste of natural resources and adds to the volume of solid waste which has to be disposed of.

Packaging is made from a variety of valuable natural resources. Cardboard is made from paper, which comes from trees, and aluminum foil comes mostly from bauxite, which is mined from the earth. Plastic, one of the most common materials used in packaging, is made from coal and oil. When we use and throw away packaging materials, we are placing great demands on our supply of natural resources.

Plastics seem to be ideal packaging materials because they are inexpensive, durable yet lightweight, and can be molded into many shapes. They can be clear or brightly colored. Also, they are not affected by moisture, sunlight, nor the action of microorganisms. The Styrofoam tray that held the pork chops was plastic. It is lightweight, yet firm enough to hold the chops without bending. The plastic wrap covering the chops was flexible so that it could wrap around the chops. It was also lightweight and could be seen through.

Since the 1940s the production of plastics has greatly increased, mainly as the result of advanced manufacturing processes. Plastics have become widely used not only in packaging, but also in many other ways. Think about all the items that you use which are made of plastic—everything from toothbrushes to raincoats.

The fact that plastics are nonbiodegradable makes their disposal a big problem. Whether plastics are disposed of on land or in water, they remain in the environment for a very long time. Plastics are almost "forever." In addition to the fact that they do not decay, they can sometimes be harmful to wildlife. Birds may get the plastic rings which hold a six-pack of soda together tightly around their necks and be unable to swallow. Hungry sea turtles may mistake plastic bags floating near the ocean's surface for jellyfish, swallow the bag, and die from intestinal blockage.

SEWAGE IN
SPARKLING WATERS

The oceans, which cover about 70 percent of the earth's surface, have been called the "last frontier" of our planet. They are a valuable resource that we are learning more and more about. Many scientists believe that the way we live in the future may be determined by how wisely we use the oceans today. The oceans could become a very important source of food, water, energy, and raw materials for the world's people.

Change often comes slowly, though, and some of the ways in which the ocean could be valuable in the future may not even be guessed at now. Doctors at Boston's Massachusetts General Hospital have only recently discovered that the skate fish, which often gets caught in fishnets, contains a chemical that is identical to one in the human brain. The skate fish, which averages a couple of feet in length and has a flattened body with winglike fins, is no longer thrown away as a "trash fish." Instead, many are given to Massachusetts General Hospital, where they are used to study chemical changes in the brain caused by anesthesia.

Many coastal cities dump their sludge into the ocean because ocean dumping costs much less than land disposal. The nation's largest dump site for sludge, The New York Bight, is located 12 nautical miles (22.1 km) offshore from New York City. Barges loaded with sludge are pulled by tug boats into the open ocean, where the sludge is dumped. In other large cities, such as San Diego and Los Angeles in California, and Boston, huge pipelines carry sludge directly out to sea. Some outfalls (outlets) are more than 6 miles (9.6 km) offshore. In 1982, 7 million tons (6.3 metric tons) of sludge from the United States were dumped into the ocean.

Because the oceans are so vast and complicated, we do not know how much sludge they can safely absorb. Sludge sometimes contains harmful chemicals and disease-carrying organisms which could be ingested by fish that are later eaten by people. The decomposers in salt water, like those in soil, break down wastes and use the nutrients as food. Then sea cucumbers, worms, clams, and other creatures eat the bacteria.

Sometimes sludge contains organisms which cannot be broken down by decomposers, or there is so much sludge that the organisms are not broken down completely. If this condition exists near shellfish beds, they must be closed because the clams, oysters, and scallops are no longer safe to eat.

The story of Boston Harbor shows how putting inadequately treated sewage into the Atlantic Ocean affects the environment. Boston Harbor, scene of the Boston Tea Party, has played a historic role in our nation's history since the days preceding the Revolutionary War. In 1779 John Adams described fishing and swimming in the "cool, tranquil and peaceful waters" around Deer Island and Moon Island, two of the harbor's islands.

The Port of Boston grew to be the largest seaport in New England and the site of one of the nation's major shipbuilding and maritime shipping industries. Thousands of people enjoyed the beautiful saltwater beaches. The thirty harbor islands were popular places to hike, fish, camp, and visit historical sites. In warm weather, pleasure boats of every description dotted the harbor. Along the waterfront, renovated brick buildings became attractive locations for people to live and work. For many reasons, Boston Harbor became special to Americans who lived near it and those who visited from far away.

Today Boston Harbor's sewage pollution problems are threatening its natural beauty. A foul odor in some places and floating debris in others affect its recreational appeal. Beaches have to be closed from time to time because of the high concentration of disease-causing bacteria. Most commercial shellfish beds are closed and millions of dollars are lost because the shellfish cannot be harvested. The kinds of organisms that normally live on the ocean floor, such as various species of worms, algae, fish, clams, lobsters, and crabs, have changed as a result of polluted waters. Some fish suffer from fin rot and others are developing cancer from poisons that have entered the water in sewage.

Every day, millions of gallons of improperly treated sewage enter Boston Harbor from the city of Boston and forty-two surrounding communities. Boston has the oldest city sewer district in the United States and it has not been upgraded to adequately treat the present volume of sewage. By 1884 most of Boston's sewage flowed by pipe to Moon Island, where it was contained in holding tanks and released untreated on the outgoing tide. Sewage treatment facilities were later built on Deer Island and Nut Island. The sludge and effluent, which receive only primary treatment from those facilities, are now discharged daily into Boston Harbor. The Moon Island tanks are in disrepair. They discharge raw sewage treated only with chlorine into Boston Harbor whenever there is a heavy rainstorm. Boston has a combined sewer system and its treatment plants are unable to manage the increased volume of water when it rains.

People, the only animals capable of complex reasoning, must make plans for Boston Harbor's rescue. Citizens must decide if they want Boston Harbor to be a place to swim, fish, and boat, and to provide food, or to carry away wastes. The

These are simulations of how Boston Harbor looked in colonial times and how it looks today. In the past **(represented in photo on left),** a wide variety of plants, invertebrates, fish, and mammals flourished in Boston Harbor. Today **(right)** deposits of decaying sludge and oily residue cover much of the harbor floor. There are many fewer kinds of organisms, but those species that have developed a tolerance to the pollution are abundant.

problems that exist are no one person's fault. When enough people regard Boston Harbor as a whole living system that must be treated with care and understanding, then the problems can be solved.

Over the years, many studies have been done on Boston Harbor and many different solutions to its pollution problems have been proposed. One was to apply to the United States Environmental Protection Agency (E.P.A.) for a special permit to build a long outfall pipe. Under this plan, sewage would receive only primary treatment. The Clean Water Act permits such arrangements in special instances when sewage can be deposited in very deep ocean waters where, it is believed, the waste will disperse and break down. A second proposed solution was to increase the capacity and capabilities of treatment plants to provide secondary treatment.

In 1985 this debate was settled by the Environmental Protection Agency. It ruled that Boston's sewage must receive secondary treatment. This decision was reached in part because it was impractical to build an outfall pipe long enough to deposit sewage in deep water. Furthermore, an outfall pipe would just change the location of the problem from Boston Harbor to Massachusetts Bay. There, thousands of pounds of decaying sewage solids deposited at the pipe's outlet would use up the oxygen that fish and other marine life need to live.

The cost of cleaning up Boston Harbor is estimated to be about two billion dollars. Some of this money may be provided by the federal government out of funds set aside to help states pay for water pollution control projects. The rest of the money may come from increased taxes or from loans. To encourage citizens to use less water, and therefore produce less wastewater, water prices might be increased. Residents might decide to install water-saving devices such as flow-restricted shower heads and toilets that require less water to flush in their houses.

There seems to be no ideal place to locate a massive sewage treatment plant to serve Boston and the other communities. Few people would choose to have one as a neighbor. They are worried that the value of their houses would go down because future buyers would not want to live near it. If the proposed location seems unfair, citizens can appeal the decision. In the United States, the courts would then decide. Although only some will live near the plant, many people must share the responsibility of restoring Boston Harbor.

About twenty years ago a situation similar to that of Boston Harbor existed in Seattle, Washington. Saltwater beaches in Elliot Bay and along Puget Sound were becoming polluted by sewage from the city's inadequate treatment plants. Fresh water in nearby Lake Washington was turning murky, and a green scum covered parts of the lake's surface. This overgrowth of algae, a small plant, resulted from excess nutrients entering the lake in sewage effluent.

When the Washington state legislature passed a law permitting local governments to join together in providing certain services, the way was cleared for the city of Seattle and the smaller surrounding towns to pool their tax revenues and services under a central government, the Municipality of Metropolitan Seattle, or "Metro." Land was purchased for construction of new sewage treatment plants and sewers. These were paid for by increases in sewer rates charged to customers. By 1983, the goal of making the waters of Seattle and surrounding communities "fishable and swimmable" had been met.

5

NEW WAYS
WITH
WASTES

As our population increases and our way of life becomes more advanced, we use more and more of our precious natural resources. It is like a seesaw with population and living standards on one end and natural resources on the other end. As our living standards and population go up, our supply of natural resources goes down. One way to lessen demand on our natural resources is to try to improve the way we use our wastes.

RECYCLING

In the future a much larger part of the wastestream may be recycled. This is a process by which the natural resources contained in refuse are used again. Perhaps we will recycle many natural resources from wastes rather than using these resources only as they are taken from the earth. In the United States today almost all our solid wastes are thrown away and never used again. In 1981, only 8 percent of solid waste was recycled.

You, unlike most people, may already be a recycler. Perhaps you make Halloween costumes from old clothes. When clothes are handed down from one child to another, they are being recycled. A student may carry a sandwich to school in the bag in which the bread was bought. Then the whole lunch is put in a paper bag that had been used before. Oatmeal boxes filled with cotton fabric scraps make good gerbil houses. Corregated cardboard boxes covered with adhesive-backed paper make storage bins for mittens and hats, games, records and tapes, and many other things. Margarine containers can be used as desk organizers to store thumbtacks and paper clips. These are just a few examples of how recycling can become a way of life.

There are other ways of recycling in which the product is actually returned to a manufacturer. We often think of products as flowing only in one direction—from the manufacturer to the consumer. We buy a beverage at the store and throw the bottle or can away when we have drunk the contents. But in recycling, products flow back in the opposite direction, from the consumer to a manufacturer. So a beverage container that is recycled goes back to a manufacturer who can reuse it, or can use the natural resources from which it is made.

The states of New York, Oregon, Vermont, Maine, Michigan, Connecticut, Iowa, Delaware, and Massachusetts have passed "bottle bills." These are laws requiring consumers to pay a deposit on beverage containers at the time of purchase. When the customer returns the empty containers to the store, the deposit is refunded. Bottle bills provide an incentive for people to dispose of beverage containers properly as well as a method of reusing the natural resources contained in them.

In states that have passed bottle bills, beverage container litter has become less of a problem. Perhaps if you live in one of these states, you have picked up a bottle or can you found on the beach, along a street, or in a wilderness area and returned it to a store. By doing this you have helped keep these areas beautiful and enabled the natural resources contained in litter to be recycled.

In some communities recycling is a project run by small groups of dedicated volunteers. They arrange with a recycling industry to place bins at the local sanitary landfill or other community location where residents can deposit recyclable materials. The first step in recycling is called source separation.

This involves separating the recyclables from the rest of the trash. The second step is sorting the recyclables. Residents deposit their clear, brown, and green glass, and newspapers and cans in the appropriate bins. Periodically the bins are emptied by the recycling industry, which pays the town for the materials. In some towns trucks collect sorted recyclables from the residents, just as garbage is collected. Some communities, such as Fresno, California, have sold one particular item to an individual industry. There, used newspapers were sold to an insulation plant which used them in the manufacture of weatherization material.

By reducing the amount of solid wastes to be disposed of, recycling may help cities and towns that are running out of places for sanitary landfills. In Massachusetts a proposal is being considered that would require people to separate recyclable materials from the rest of their trash. If this were not done, their trash would not be collected. Glass, paper, and cans would be picked up at the curbside and brought to regional collection centers. There these recyclables would be further sorted and crushed or cleaned. Finally, they would be sold to industries which would reuse their raw materials.

Even household wastes that are hazardous can be recycled. When a car's oil is changed, the used motor oil must be discarded. Because it is flammable, it is not safe to put in the trash. Many recycling centers have a large container where used oil is collected. In many states, such as New York, used oil can be returned to a gas station. Oil companies buy back the oil and employ it for industrial uses that do not require a high grade of oil.

Colorado's Governor Richard Lamm is shown here using an aluminum recycling machine at a Denver supermarket. The machine gives customers twenty-four cents for each pound of old aluminum cans.

In some places in the United States, Canada, and other industrialized nations, there are salvage systems in which many kinds of materials are recycled. Used paper is returned to paper mills where the ink is removed and the paper is reformed. (Perhaps you have seen recycled paper—it is sometimes marked with a symbol which you can find on some greeting cards, cereal cartons, and cardboard boxes.) When paper is recycled, trees are saved from being cut down. Iron and steel are returned to foundries, and aluminum and other metals are melted down for new products at smelters. Scrap glass is ground and used to make new glass, or it can be used in the manufacture of insulation and road building materials. Discarded tires are shredded into "crumb rubber" and used to make asphalt to construct and repair roads. Garbage and leaves are sent to composting plants to make humus.

COMPOSTING

Composting is a method to speed up the natural process of decay, and has been practiced for centuries. Long ago people knew that straw soaked in barnyard wastes and then spread on planted fields helped crops to grow. Trees were fertilized by filling holes dug around their roots with wood ashes and manure. This mixture of plant and animal matter provided the trees with nutrients. The word *compost*, which means to mix together once-living things, comes from the word "compote," meaning to mix together, to stew.

Today many gardeners have compost piles in their yards. They save garbage scraps such as vegetable and fruit peelings, eggshells, and coffee grounds as well as leaves and lawn clippings. These items are put on the compost pile and covered with soil. After about three to six months the composted materials become humus. This is a brown or black material that has the texture of coarse bread crumbs. Along with providing nutrients, humus acts like a sponge. It enriches the topsoil, helps it hold water during a dry spell, and prevents it from washing away in a rainstorm. Composting occurs naturally in dumps and sanitary landfills. The decomposers break down the solid wastes that were made from once-living things.

WATER CONSERVATION
AND SEWAGE

Water, like topsoil, is one of our most precious natural resources. For centuries, people have depended on water, not only for drinking, but also for irrigating farms, for cleaning and cooking, for carrying away wastes in sewage, for recreation, and for manufacturing. Now, with increasing population and modern standards of living, we are using so much water that the water level in some *reservoirs* and wells is beginning to be drawn down. The amount of pure drinking water we are using is greater than can be replaced by rain and snowfall.

One way to help prevent water shortages is to consider plumbing systems that conserve water. Toilets do not need to be flushed with water that is pure enough to drink. Instead, households could reuse water that has first been used for other purposes. Wastewater from the washing machine, dishwasher, bathroom sink, shower, and bathtub is polluted only lightly, and is called "greywater." It could be reused to flush toilets. The Lavatory-Toilet has been designed to do just that. It has a faucet located above the toilet tank. When you wash your hands or brush your teeth, the dirty water flows into a standard washbasin fit into the toilet tank. This water, instead of flowing through a drain into a sewage system, goes directly into the toilet tank. Then the greywater, rather than fresh water, is used to flush the toilet.

The wastewater from the toilet is called "blackwater." It contains urine, feces, and bacteria which may cause disease. It cannot be reused unless it is purified. Because the wastewater from the kitchen sink contains grease and high concentrations of soap and food particles, it can clog pipes and produce odors. For these reasons this water, like blackwater, should flow into a sewage system. Plumbing in most American houses mixes blackwater and greywater. Perhaps as people become more aware of the need to save our drinking water supplies, greywater plumbing systems will become more common. Then greywater from bathtubs, showers, and washing machines could be piped to a large tank where it would be held until it was needed for tasks such as watering lawns or washing cars.

Existing toilets can be modified so that they will use less than five gallons (19 l) of water with every flush. A hardened brick (the kind that will not break up in water) or a plastic bottle filled with pebbles can be put into the toilet tank. These take up space which would normally be filled with water. Yet the flushing action of the toilet remains adequate.

Some European and Japanese toilets differ greatly from the version of the flush toilet with which we are familiar. The lever on these toilets has two positions: one to flush feces; the other to flush only urine, which requires much less water. Another kind of toilet, the compressed air toilet, uses only about two quarts (1.9 l) of water per flush. It flushes effectively because water which is under pressure flows rapidly from the toilet tank.

DRY TOILETS

The "sausage" toilet of Swedish design seals and freezes human wastes in removable plastic wrappings. Incineration toilets such as the "destrolet" operate by electricity or natural gas. When the toilet bowl lid is down, the wastes are burned. Although these dry toilets conserve water, petroleum is used in the manufacture of plastic wrappings, and energy is burned in the incineration process.

Biological toilets also do not require water. They digest human waste products and kitchen garbage through the natural process of decay. Some have an electric heating unit to raise the temperature and speed up decomposition. A ventilation pipe to the outside ensures an adequate flow of air to the decaying matter and carries away odors.

The Clivus Multrum is a Swedish composting toilet. It has a wide pipe under the toilet seat connecting to a specially designed tank below which collects wastes. A separate chute connecting to the same tank is used to dispose of kitchen wastes. Other once-living things such as sawdust or dry shredded leaves can also be added. There is no electric heater, but whenever possible solar heat is used to warm the air that circulates in the tank. As the contents decompose by the action of bacteria and other microorganisms, the volume of wastes is greatly reduced. The humus that is produced can be used for fertilizer on garden plants and those vegetables that are not root crops. The liquid that is produced by the Clivus tank is of high nitrogen content and is also an excellent fertilizer.

AQUACULTURE

New kinds of sewage treatment plants as well as new designs in bathroom fixtures are being created in an effort to conserve water. Research at the National Air and Space Administration's (NASA's) National Space Technology Laboratories has shown that aquaculture can remove pollutants from sewage and purify the wastewater. The acquaculture process involves using wastes of one life-form as food for another life-form. The plant chosen for NASA's aquaculture was the water hyacinth *(Eichhornia crassipes)*. It is a tropical plant that grows in Central and South America and parts of the southern United States. It has stalklike leaves and produces attractive purple flowers. These parts of the plant float on the surface. The extensive root system is underwater. The water hyacinth is found in almost all of Florida's lakes and rivers. In many places it has become a nuisance because it reproduces so rapidly that sometimes these mats of floating "weeds" choke out other kinds of plants and get in the way of boaters.

At EPCOT (Experimental Prototype Community of Tomorrow), Walt Disney World, Florida, a model water hyacinth wastewater treatment plant has been built. First the wastewater flows into a tank called the primary clarifier. Here some of the solids settle out as sludge. Next the wastewater flows into the water hyacinth channels. The action of bacteria breaks down compounds in the sewage into simpler substances. These are taken up by the hyacinths and used as food. Together with sunlight, these nutrients enable the plants to grow and reproduce. After five to six days the wastewater reaches the end of the hyacinth channels. The water is clearer, wastes in the water are reduced, and the effluent meets water treatment standards.

Mature water hyacinths are harvested from time to time in order to promote growth of younger ones. The harvested plants are cut up in a chopper and then ground to make them even smaller. Together with sludge from the primary clarifier, some of the ground hyacinths are put into a tank called a digester, where there is no air. As this mixture is broken down by bacteria, methane and carbon dioxide gases are produced. The methane, which is like natural gas, is used as a source of energy. The harvested hyacinths are also used for mulch, fertilizer, and animal fodder.

If you visited one of San Diego, California's sewage treatment plants, it would look like a series of greenhouses for water hyacinths. This expanding city of nearly one million people has such a low amount of rainfall per year that almost all of its water is piped in from far away. Its goal is to be one of the first cities in the nation to be able to provide its citizens with quality drinking water—from sewage.

San Diego's demonstration aquaculture project began in 1981. It was designed to copy nature's method of treating wastes by creating a swamp in a tank. First a layer of muck from a local swamp is spread over the bottom of six tanks. Species of animals that live in a natural swamp—such as snails, crayfish, and worms—are added to some of the tanks. Duck-

The Water Utilities Department of San Diego, California, uses water hyacinths for sewage treatment because of the plants' ability to absorb and metabolize pollutants. The flowers thrive on a sludge diet.

weed, a tiny, green plant, keeps down the growth of algae. The tanks are also stocked with gambusia fish to eat mosquito larvae.

Water hyacinths are grown in each of the tanks. They are planted sparsely to allow room for new plants to sprout. By planting one-quarter of the area, water hyacinths spread to cover the tank completely in four to eight weeks. Then partial harvesting occurs, leaving about one-quarter of the plants in place. (A study is being done to determine if the harvested hyacinths can be safely fed to beef cattle and chickens and used as fertilizer on edible plants.) To prevent water hyacinths from becoming inactive during the winter months, enclosed plastic greenhouses keep the temperature constant. Air is pumped into the hyacinth tanks to control odors that build up in the swamplike atmosphere.

Sewage flows into the first three aquaculture tanks at the same time. Next it goes into tanks four, five, and six. When it leaves the sixth tank, the effluent is purer than after traditional secondary sewage treatment. In a process called reverse osmosis, the water flows through a very fine filter that removes salt and viruses. Future plans call for this water to be further treated by holding it in specially designated lakes. When it is restored to drinking water quality, it will become part of San Diego's water supply.

NEW WAYS WITH SEWAGE ACROSS THE UNITED STATES

Tucson, Arizona, is another western city that is trying to reuse its sewage to avoid water shortages. The Santa Cruz riverbed runs through the west side of this desert city. Before 1940, parts of the river ran continuously, but since that time the riverbed carries water only after a rainstorm. Water birds such as herons left the exposed rocks and mud flats in search of flowing water elsewhere. With the loss of surface water, all of the city's water now had to be provided from underground *aquifers*. Huge quantities of water were pumped out of the aquifers for households, golf courses, farms, and use in copper mines. Many more houses were built, and owners planted large lawns and species of trees (such as mulberry) that are not native to the dry Southwest. Such types and amounts of plant life need much more water than plants that normally grow in desert regions. And, despite rapid evaporation of water in the hot climate, thousands of backyard swimming pools which required constant refilling were built. As a result of all these activities, the water table dropped by 180 feet (54 m) in some areas.

Tucson, in addition to looking for more water resources, plans to spend 35 million dollars over the next ten years for the development of a system using sewage effluent to irrigate parks, cemeteries, and golf courses. At the present time, this effluent is discharged from the city's two sewage treatment plants and carried away. Officials hope that charging higher prices for water will encourage residents to use less by installing water-saving toilets, using swimming pool covers, and planting yards with less grass and more desert plants. In the future, Tucson may opt for recycling sewage effluent for drinking water.

Santee, California, a city of 60,000 people 20 miles (32 km) northeast of San Diego, uses its wastewater for recreation. People paddle canoes, row boats, and fish in the Santee Lakes, which were created out of wastewater from sewage. The story of how the Santee Lakes came into being goes back to the years before World War II when Santee was a rural farming community. Because it received only ten inches (25 cm) of rainfall a year, farmers depended on the nearby San Diego River to provide water for irrigation. Even when the river dried up during the hot summer months, a large underground aquifer supplied enough water for people, dairy cattle, and crops.

As San Diego grew, its residents required more and more water, and so the El Capitan Dam was built on the San Diego River. The huge reservoir that was created behind it supplied water to San Diego. The dam kept water from flowing in the San Diego River, thereby reducing the level of water underground. There was no longer sufficient water for Santee, and wells had to be dug deeper and deeper to find water. At these depths, water became salty and was unhealthy for crops. Soon even these underground sources went dry and people sold their farms. The herds of cattle and fields of alfalfa and corn were replaced by thousands of new houses for people who had come to Southern California to find jobs. Santee and the entire Southern California area continued to grow and needed yet an additional source of water to meet increasing demands. An aqueduct more than 240 miles (384 km) long was built to carry water from the Colorado River west to this region.

In the late 1950s another water problem arose. California laws raised the purity standards for effluent being dumped into its inland waterways. Santee could no longer dump its wastewater into Sycamore Canyon Creek, a branch of the San Diego River, even though it had received secondary treatment. There seemed to be only two possible solutions, both of which would be very expensive. One was to further treat the sewage, but methods for doing this were still experimental. The second option was for Santee to sign a forty-year contract to become a member of the Metropolitan Sewer System and join San Diego in dumping effluent into the Pacific Ocean.

The manager of the Santee County Water District, realizing that sewage is composed of 99.9 percent water, urged community leaders to consider reclaiming this water and using it again. The existing sewage treatment plant was located at the mouth of the shallow Sycamore Canyon, which had gentle sloping sides and a bottom of clay covered with layers of sand and gravel. Much of the land within this canyon was scarred and pitted by a sand and gravel mining operation on the site. The manager's idea was to transform the pits into beautiful lakes. He met with the owner of the Sycamore Canyon land, who was enthusiastic about the plan and who agreed to donate his land for the project.

However, many Santee residents thought the plan to use purified wastewater for recreational purposes was a joke. Public meetings were held to explain how the creation of these lakes could benefit people and how the wastewater would be treated.

First, the wastewater would receive primary and secondary treatment in a sewage treatment plant. It would then flow to an oxidation pond where decomposers would interact with the water and continue to cleanse it. Then the effluent would be pumped up the canyon, where it would be put into shallow basins. As it filtered through layers of sand and gravel, it would be further purified. Finally, the now crystal clear water would flow into the uppermost of a numbered chain of lakes.

Public health agencies wanted to be sure that disease-causing bacteria and viruses were no longer present in the reclaimed water. Tests were performed on the water to see if these organisms had been successfully controlled. Finally the lakes were determined safe enough for boating and in June 1961, the Festival of the Lakes was held to celebrate their opening. People were joyful about the removal of high fences, which had kept them away from the inviting lakes. Citizens who had been critical of the project in the beginning were now impatient to be able to enjoy the lakes.

In 1965 a team of experts from across the United States determined that it was safe to open a swimming pool which was filled with additionally treated water from the Santee Lakes. A nine-year-old became the first person in the nation to swim in reclaimed sewage water. Today the seven Santee Lakes attract thousands of visitors who enjoy boating, swimming, fishing, and overnight camping. This series of lakes in an otherwise dry area has proved that water is too valuable a resource to be used once and thrown away.

The Santee Wastewater Reclamation Project was designed to treat one million gallons (3.8 million l) of sewage a day. As the city has grown, the amount of sewage has exceeded this capacity. To handle the additional volume, Santee had to connect to the San Diego Metropolitan Sewage System.

DECISION MAKING
IN A DEMOCRACY

Waste management is no longer of interest only to trash collectors. Research in this field is being conducted by marine biologists, university scientists, private industry, wildlife specialists, and all levels of government. Experts in all areas have come to realize that there really is no such place as "away." Our planet has only a limited amount of space and resources. The places we throw our wastes are the same places that we depend on for the water we drink, the food we eat, and the air we breathe. All of our achievements in science and technology have served to remind us that people do not exist outside of nature, but are part of it. We must learn to make use of our waste products as other species do, for wastes are part of the cycle of life. They are too valuable a natural resource to continue throwing away.

GLOSSARY

aerobes— organisms that can only live in the presence of oxygen.

anaerobes— organisms that can only live in the absence of oxygen.

aqueduct— a pipe or other channel that carries water over a long distance.

aquifer— an underground layer of rock, usually composed of gravel or porous stone, that contains water.

biodegradable— capable of being broken down into harmless products by the action of decomposers.

cesspit— an underground pit into which household sewage is deposited.

compost— a mixture of decaying material that was once living.

decompose— to rot or decay; to break down through chemical change into simple compounds.

effluent— a discharge of pollutants into the environment. These are partially or completely treated or in their natural state.

latrine— a pit in the earth that is used as a toilet.

leachate— liquid, often rainwater, that has passed through solid waste or other substances and then carries with it dissolved or suspended materials.

microorganism— an organism that is too small to be seen by the naked eye.

nutrient— a substance or ingredient that provides nourishment and is needed for growth.

obsolete— no longer inuse, outmoded by newer types or designs.

organism— an individual living plant or animal.

privy— a toilet without plumbing.

refuse— something that is discarded as rubbish, garbage, or trash.

reservoir— a place, such as an artificial lake, where large amounts of water are stored.

sewage— the total of bodily wastes and wastewater produced by residences, businesses, farms, and industries.

sludge— a semi-liquid substance consisting of solids and wastewater that is produced as a result of sewage treatment.

solid waste— unwanted, discarded material that does not contain enough liquid to flow freely.

wastestream— the total waste output from an area or a facility.

wastewater— water carrying dissolved or suspended solids from homes, farms, businesses, or industries.

INDEX